THE REMAINING
FACTORS

Seeking Eternal Treasures

David R. Allen

authorHOUSE®

AuthorHouse™
1663 Liberty Drive, Suite 200
Bloomington, IN 47403
www.authorhouse.com
Phone: 1-800-839-8640

First published by AuthorHouse 1/5/2009

ISBN: 978-1-4389-4392-3 (sc)

Printed in the United States of America
Bloomington, Indiana

This book is printed on acid-free paper.

*All scripture quotes are taken from
The New Revised Standard Version*

May Jesus Christ Be Glorified and His Kingdom Increase!

I dedicate "**The Remaining Factors**" to my wife, Lotte, and my children, Grant and Paige.

Special thanks to my mother, who made this publication possible.

To Sandra Wahl, the cover artist.
To Linda Norris, my editor.

CONTENTS

INTRODUCTION   vii

CHAPTER 1:   DIVISION   1

CHAPTER 2:   THE HOPE FACTOR   9

CHAPTER 3:   THE FAITH FACTOR   17

CHAPTER 4:   THE LOVE FACTOR   35

CHAPTER 5:   TESTIMONY   47

CHAPTER 6:   CALL TO REACTION   53

INTRODUCTION

I grew up in a Christian home. My parents were evangelists and each of them had a genuine faith relationship with God. My father had a passion for the Word of God and thoroughly enjoyed preaching. Mother was born with a gift for music. She wrote and recorded two albums of spiritual songs, along with other great accomplishments in music. So, as a result of my upbringing, I always had knowledge of the ways of the Lord and loved Him. When I was eight years old, my parents divorced and my relationship with God became non-existent.

I knew all about the salvation God gave the world by means of His Son, Jesus. I had prayed a sinner's prayer many times, and I always meant to repent. My life would change for a day or a week, but it never lasted. This was the condition of my heart after my father left. At one point in my life, I was deeply entangled in sin and had said in my heart that I did not need God. In fact, I thought I was better than

God. I was popular and had many girlfriends. I enjoyed smoking, drinking, cursing, and gambling. Every moment of every day was lived in pursuit of selfish pleasure. My life contained no real concern for anyone except myself.

On October 13, 1993 my life changed forever. A girl who lived up the road from my house asked me to take her to the store to buy cigarettes. Maybe I felt generous this day? I do not really know why, but I must have agreed, because that is where we were coming from when it happened. We were in traffic and it was moving slowly. Being the impatient person I was, I decided to take a back road so I could pick up speed. The road I detoured on had a speed limit of 25 mph. Police say I must have been moving at about 80 mph when my front tires went over a pile of gravel on the side of the road. This sent my car airborne and upside down onto the side of a hill. My head smashed into the windshield which caused my brain to hemorrhage.

The police had to cut open the car to rescue our bodies from the collision. The girl riding alongside me broke her hip. As for me, I was transported from the wreck by helicopter to ICU at Allegheny General Hospital. Immediately, I went into a coma for two weeks, so the details I am giving you are from the people who cared for me. My family prayed for my life unceasingly as I remained in critical condition, having the fluids drained from my brain which had ruptured. The doctors did not expect me to survive.

After three days my brain stopped hemorrhaging. The doctors said I would live but probably remain comatose. Ten days later I awoke from the coma. When I awoke my body was completely changed. I could no longer walk, talk, eat, or see. The right half of my body suffered nerve damage resulting in paralysis. The left half had lost all motor skills, which left me with no coordination. Like all brain damaged people, I also suffered a loss of memory. In my case the loss was strictly the short term memory. Every memory I had ever accumulated throughout my life was still stored, including all the education I had at this point. It was my short term memory which had been affected. This meant that I was incapable of learning new information.

The next three months of my life were spent as an in-patient at a rehabilitation hospital. Monday through Saturday I was treated with physical, occupational, speech, and recreational therapy. I took physical and speech twice a day. Almost all of the patients there had head injuries. Many of them were confused and all of us were unrealistic about recovery. Maybe we were all just in denial, but there seemed to be a lot of positive energy there. I really believed that life would continue just as it was before I had this accident and nothing would change. Therefore, I was very optimistic and eagerly anticipated returning home to continue the wild lifestyle that I had been pulled away from.

Although I was hopeful, reality was different. The doctors were not satisfied with my progress and were beginning to see little improvement. I still could not walk, and my motor skills had made little improvement. My speech was very limited and my short term memory was still missing. They told my mother that I had plateaued and did not think I would be able to care for myself. They recommended that I be admitted into a nursing home. My mother had more faith and told the doctors that between her and my sixteen year old sister, I would have around the clock care at home. Against their better judgment, the doctors agreed to allow me to go home. How happy this made me that my old life was being restored; at least that's what I thought.

It was Christmas Eve 1993 when I returned home. On Christmas day my friends came over to see me. I thought everything would be the same as before. They were all so nice and told stories of how they missed me. As they left that day, my hope was supercharged to continue healing so I could return to my old life. But I seldom saw any of them ever again. By January, I began outpatient rehabilitation. Come April, I had plateaued again and still made little progress. The therapist thought I was probably not going to ever improve much more, and therefore they could not ask for more funding. By this time my friends never visited anymore.

At this point in my life, I was becoming desperate for a miracle. Being raised in a Christian home I knew all about God, even though I did not really know Him personally. I had spent my whole life in churches and other Christian settings. I knew that God had the power to heal me. I said a prayer and tried to make a bargain with God. Smoking was a habit I continued even after this horrible accident. Wittingly, I told God that I would quit smoking, and in appreciation, He should heal me. The next day, around noon, shortly after lunch, I was smoking a cigarette. Immediately, I was filled with sorrow and regret. Because I had repented so many times as a kid, I knew that God is real and He is supreme. I also knew that you do not break a promise or lie to God. What had I done now? All day long I contemplated the consequences of my actions. I figured that not only would I never be healed now but also that I was going to hell for sure. This was rock bottom in my mind, unforgivable. I cried to my mother all day long. That night, she called her brother and asked me to talk with him. He told me it would be all right and encouraged me to read Romans, Chapter 8. Even though I had read parts of the Bible before and it always seemed powerless, my uncle was a man of God and a missionary in Jamaica. So, I took his advice.

When I read Romans 8, for the first time in my life there was power in the Scripture. From the start of the chapter, it tells about an escape from life in the flesh. To me this meant that I could escape smoking. Also, it reads that this escape is through life according to the Spirit in Christ. At that moment it was the conclusion that really spoke to me. Romans 8: 38, 39 reads, "For I am convinced that neither death, nor life, nor angels, nor rulers, nor things present, nor things to come, nor powers, nor height, nor depth, nor anything else in all creation, will be able to separate us from the love of God in Christ Jesus our Lord." In a word, that sealed the deal for me. Here I was, completely shaken up by my sin. I read that there is a love of God that guarantees victory and is inseparable. So, I read it again, and it hit me that all this is in Christ Jesus. It was not in me or anything I could do or have done. It's a love of God that is totally dependent on Jesus and what He has done. I always knew this, but it really took me exhausting my every effort to please God on my own for me to really see just how dependent on Jesus salvation is.

It was at this point that my life began to dramatically change. A new and living hope had inspired and empowered me to begin praying, reading the Bible, and attending church and Bible studies. My heart became saturated with an unending love. I began confessing the name of Jesus Christ where ever I went, and the Holy Spirit began healing my body.

My speech began to greatly improve, and I even began preaching the word. God moved me from a walker, to a cane, to walking on my own. He also renewed my mind with His word. The doctors said I would not be able to return to school, but I did return and graduated from an accelerated class. I never had any talent or education in music, but the Holy Spirit began to fill my mind with songs of praise. When I was 19, my mother supported me in recording a number of the songs God had inspired me with.

The next four years of my life are a powerful testimony of what a life in Jesus can achieve. I was invited to speak in many churches, campgrounds, and various Christian organizations. I ministered in the U.S. and foreign nations such as Canada, Jamaica, and Spain. My face was seen in newspapers and on television, and my voice was heard on radio. At this point I had big plans to serve God as a pastor; I had been accepted into Asbury College which is well known for their Bible/theology education. It was evident to everyone who knew me that I had the call of God on my life.

The year I planned to leave for college, I met a girl and let her have my heart. Over the next five months our relationship was pulling me down. I saw her every day, and we went to church less often each month. I became more interested in pleasing her than God. God warned me about this relationship, but I hardened my heart. As a result, I was in a three-year marriage that ended in divorce. Four months later, the divorce was final under terms of irreconcilable differences. I was very hurt, but I still longed for a bride.

Immediately upon my divorce I began to seek God out again and His help in finding love. I prayed very specifically for a beautiful, kind, gentle, smart, godly, Asian woman who would love and remain faithful to me always. These are just some of the things I asked for in my wife. The next four months I became obsessed with this dream. I spent every waking hour chatting on the internet, trying to find this woman. Four months after my divorce was final, I met a Philippine woman on a Christian matchmaker website. She was a very strong Christian and truly loved the Lord. I had never seen her but was confident that she was God's choice. I told her to come to Pittsburgh and see me. She said she would pray about it and let me know. I went to a revival for the next three days to seek God. I felt Him assure me about her as I sought Him out. When I returned home, she had emailed me that she felt God told her to come to Pittsburgh. Now, I was fully convicted that she was God's choice for me, so I offered to buy her a plane ticket. She agreed to come for one week before she had to return home.

When I saw her, it was incredible how she met the specifications of my prayers. As she was on the plane to Pittsburgh, God spoke to her through His word from the book of Ruth. This is the word she received: "Where you go, I will go; where you lodge, I will lodge; your people shall be my people, And your God my God" (Ruth 1:16). So, when I proposed after only three days, she was already prepared to say yes. My first marriage was a painful relationship and a direct act of disobedience toward God. My present marriage is a joyful blessing and a gracious gift of that inseparable love of God which is only in Christ Jesus, my Lord. It most definitely is a gift of His graces, because after the first marriage, I definitely did not deserve a wife that was so specific to my requests.

The first two years of our marriage were the perfect minister to promote healing in my relationship with God. My faith was becoming stronger every day. I was working hard and being promoted at work. About three months after my promotion, I fell at work and fractured my ankle. The company doctor misdiagnosed my fracture and treated the injury as a sprain. A fracture and a sprain are supposed to be treated differently. A sprain is worked and a fracture is rested. As a result of the mistreatment, my ankle developed arthritis. This resulted in a lifetime of sedentary duty. The grocery store I worked for quietly placed me in the video department located in a closed corner of the store. At first I thought this was a blessing, and maybe it was, but the longer I was there, the darker my life became. They assigned me to work the lottery machine, and I became a gambler and lover of money. Movie rentals were free, and so I would watch every movie and became a lover of pleasure. I began collecting movies and I treasured my collection. Because I was on sedentary duty all day long, I also became lazy and constantly desired more. I could not hear from God anymore because I was weighed down with the cares of the world.

After about three years of this, I realized how dark my life had become, and I was powerless to escape. Over this time, my loving and caring wife had blessed me with two beautiful children. I realized that if something were to happen to me that the only memory they would have of me was a man who sought to continually please and gratify the flesh. At that moment I cried out to God to save me from myself. I cried and said that I was weak and enjoyed these things too much to possibly give them up. I begged God to help me escape before I died in my sin. I would like to tell you that my life magically changed at that moment, but it didn't. What did change was my heart. Over the next month the cares of this world, allure of wealth, and the desire for other things began to dissolve. The eternal things became greater every day. Don't think it was instantaneous like when I was saved. No, I had to go through a time of separation, and it was painful. Nevertheless,

God was mighty to deliver me after I determined to set my heart on things above.

As I look back at life, there seems to be one common thread linking all my troubles. That thread is the condition of my heart. No matter how hard my heart becomes, faith, hope, and love always continue. This hope has carried me. This faith has empowered me. His love has suspended me. 1 Corinthians 13:13 reads, "And now faith, hope, and love abide." I like to call these three the remaining factors. Every time I tried to get close to God, the cares of this world, the lure of wealth, and the desire for other things would bring me to harden my heart toward God.

As you read this book, let it inspire you to hope. Let it give you patience to persevere in faith. Most importantly, let it teach you to love. It is my prayer that these chapters will inspire believers to become more mature in Christ. If the reader does not know Christ, then my prayer is that this book will ignite a desire to be transformed. May God bless you and keep you always.

CHAPTER 1:

DIVISION

"Do you think I have come to bring peace to the earth? No, I tell you, but rather division!"

(Luke 12:51)

While reading this chapter, consider the future return of Christ. Know that this world and the things of it are passing away. Make a decision today to live a life separate from this world and begin to focus on eternal treasures with hope, faith, and love.

THE SOBERING TRUTH

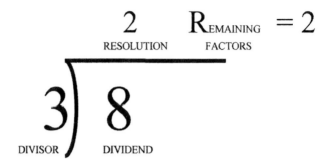

In the mathematical world of long division, there are three components to every math problem. These components have names. First, there is the dividend, which is the unit that is to be divided. Second, there is the divisor, which is the dividing unit. Third, there is the resolution, which is the end unit of a resolved problem. Often when a problem is resolved, the end unit does not come out evenly. Parts exist which make the end unit whole. These existing parts are called the remaining factors.

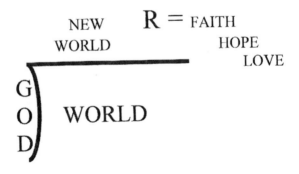

In the same way, think of the world as the dividend and the mystery of God as the divisor. In Romans 3:9-20 the Bible tells us of a "sin problem" in the world. As a result the world is being divided. The world will be divided into believers and unbelievers. The unbelievers will be thrown into the lake of fire and destroyed (see Revelation 21:8). The believers will dwell in a new world with God for all eternity (see Revelation 21:7). This new world is the glorious end unit of the resolved problem of sin. We will dwell with God and God with us. Sin and its effects will no longer be a problem.

The thirteenth chapter of Corinthians tells about the supremacy of love over all other parts of spiritual service. These parts are called spiritual gifts, for they are merely reflections of the whole. The whole is the mystery of God, and remember, "God is love" (1 John 4:8). Therefore, the gift of love is the greatest reflection of God in the believer. Love is the greatest, but when the mystery of God has been resolved, three reflections will continue to exist: faith, hope, and love; these will be the remaining factors. Therefore, "Cast all your anxiety on him, because he cares for you. Discipline yourselves, keep alert. Like a roaring lion, your adversary, the devil prowls around, looking for someone to devour. Resist him, steadfast in your faith" (1 Peter 5: 7, 8, 9).

THE DIVISOR

The divisor has been identified as the dividing unit. When referring to the problem of sin in the world, the divisor is the mystery of God. God is a holy God. Yes, God is a holy, holy God! Revelation 4:8 reads, "Holy, holy, holy, the Lord God the Almighty." He is also a perfectly just God. He is given the title "Righteous Judge" in 2 Timothy 4:8. This means that He cannot tolerate sin either morally or ethically. That creates a problem if every person is a sinner. God wants to dwell with us, but the sin in our lives makes this seem impossible. It was Jesus who in 2 Corinthians 5:21 was, "… to be one who knew no sin, so that in him we might become the righteousness of God." This is the means of salvation given to those who believe. The Bible tells us that God is sending Jesus a second time to resolve the problem He began dividing. Luke 12:52 records this division: "from now on five in a household will be divided, three against two and two against three." One thing there is to be sure of; when the problem is resolved, the resolution will not contain any mistakes. Be sure to be part of this grand resolution.

THE DIVIDEND

The dividend has been defined as the unit being divided. Again, because of sin, it is the world that is being divided. There is no escape from the consequences of sin. For Romans 6:23 clearly informs that "the wages of sin is death." Ultimately, this division will bring ruin to this world. This is nothing new. In Matthew 12:25 Jesus tells the Pharisees, "'Every kingdom divided against itself is laid waste." God is the divisor, but division is within the world. The division is the believer/unbeliever, righteousness/wickedness, godly/ungodly and the like. The dividing line is clear and so are the results, life/death. Jesus said in Revelation 16:15, "See, I am coming like a thief! Blessed is he who stays awake." Yes, Jesus is coming again when the world will not expect. So, prepare by living a life separated from the world and pleasing to God.

THE RESOLUTION

Finally, when this problem is resolved, Heaven and Earth will be recreated. At last, the mystery of God will be revealed and perfection will have come. Only those people on God's side of the dividing line will continue to exist. They will live with Jesus in this new world. After all this, there is one thing to be certain of. 1 Corinthians 13:10 reads, "But when the complete comes, the partial will come to an end" and only three will continue. That's right. We cannot take our riches, possessions, or any earthly treasure with us. We can store up eternal treasures in Heaven by keeping hold of hope, faith, and love which will abide. "For where your treasure is, there your heart will be also" (Matthew 6:21).

TREASURES

What a privilege we have being gifted with three eternal functions. Having these abilities and knowing they will abide forever should inspire us to impart them into others. For it stands to reason that anyone we would want to see in eternity would also need to possess hope in God, faith in God, and the love of God to abide. Simply replace the noun (God) with the proper noun (Jesus), and the Gospel message is present.

Those people whom we treasure most are the people that we should be most determined to show God's reflection in us. Reflect God with every gift He has given you, especially hope, faith, and love. For these three are guaranteed to build up eternal treasures when the heart is set on things above. If a person has the ability for throwing a 100 mph fastball with perfect aim, he or she would most likely try to use that gift. He might become a major league pitcher and build up wealth with that gift. Just think about the worldly goods this one gift can achieve. Now, consider the heavenly treasures that a believer can achieve being equipped with three gifts. Paul warned Timothy, "Do not neglect the gift that is in you" (1 Timothy 4:14). What Paul was saying is do not fail to care for the gift and let it be idle. If a pitcher does not care for his arm or work it out regularly, he will become weak and ineffective. Do not become weak and ineffective in eternal things. Rather choose to put into practice the remaining factors to multiply and increase what will be revealed.

CHAPTER 2:

THE HOPE FACTOR

"The Lord is my portion," says my soul,
"therefore I will hope in Him."
(Lamentations 3:24)

L et this chapter redirect our dreams and visions to the only eternal source where there is full assurance.

HOPE DEFINED

The Apostle Peter gives Christians a picture of "Satan on the prowl like an angry lion looking for a way to swallow them whole. He tells them to hope in the Lord while watching with self control so they will be able to stand in the faith" (paraphrase of 1 Peter 5:7, 8, 9). Satan wants to destroy the hope we have in Christ. Hope is a critical element in our faith. Hope is the only element that a believer has any control over. The reason hope is in their control is because hope is the desire of expectation.

An old joke goes, a little girl was praying to God one night before bed, when her mother heard her saying, "and please, Lord, let Charles Dickens be the author of *Romeo and Juliet*!!!"

When her mother heard this, she asked her why she asked God for that.

The little girl cried out, "Because that's the answer I wrote down on my literature test."

As silly as this little girl's hope is, it perfectly illustrates that what she desires to happen is her hope. Webster's dictionary defines hope as "a feeling that what is wanted will happen."

REASONS TO HOPE

Why then is hope so important? One reason is because hope is a gift from God. 1 Corinthians 13 informs Christians that hope is one of the three gifts that will remain eternally. This is hope as it is mentioned in the Bible. There is a worldly hope which exists in the sinful desires of the heart. An example of this would be the hope of divorce when a marriage is not as happy as was expected. Truly, this kind of hope leaves people in despair with uncertainty. Many people play the lottery in hope of fast and easy fortune. People are so willing to invest in worldly hope which is temporal and always disappoints. There is no assurance in this worldly hope.

God's gift of hope is rooted in a greater gift. Hope is rooted in the greatest gift of all, which is true *agape* love. This love "hopes all things." There is full assurance in this hope because "love never ends." As Paul writes, "hope does not disappoint us, because God's love has been poured out in our hearts" (Romans 5:5). As a result, all hope that is based in God's love is confident. Later, we will read that love makes all the gifts work. This is not a "hope it and have it" promise or law. No, actually this is a promise of patient endurance while in expectation through love. 1 Corinthians 13 also points out "love is patient and endures all things."

When ministered correctly, a spiritual gift should build up the body of Christ. Edification is the purpose of all spiritual gifts. The gift of hope is to edify believers with dreams and visions. It is important to use wisdom in discerning hope. This does not mean a crazy dream cannot be of God, but if a crazy dream is of God, it will line up with the Spirit. Therefore, know God's Spirit and how He operates. 1 Corinthians 12:3 reads, "understand that no one speaking by the Spirit of God ever says 'let Jesus be accursed,' and no one can say "Jesus is Lord' except by the Holy Spirit." The surest source for understanding God's Spirit is the infallible Word. Hope that is from God's Spirit will never contradict Scripture.

Another reason hope is so important is because it is essential to the spreading of the Gospel. The Gospel is the good news. The Gospel is full of expectation in things like redemption, justification, sanctification, and glorification. 1 Peter 3:15 instructs, "Always be ready to make your defense to anyone who demands from you an accounting for the hope that is in you." This is one of the reasons that Christians stop witnessing. They have stopped hoping. What happens to a person when he or she loses hope? They become cold, bitter, depressed, and altogether negative. Never give up hoping in the Lord.

A third reason hope is so important is that there are two elements to faith according to Hebrews 11:1. The first is "the assurance of things hoped for." Assurance has already been identified in hope that is found in the love of God. Two words that adequately define assurance, as it is used here, are reasonable confidence. If Satan can somehow change a reasonable confidence into an uncertainty or doubt, all assurance is lost. The hope has been contaminated with doubt and unbelief. When assurance is lost, hope has lost the core of what sets it apart from worldly hope. Worldly hope cannot produce God- pleasing faith. Hebrews 10:35 instructs, "Do not, therefore, abandon that confidence of yours."

Understand that reasonable confidence promotes belief, but in itself is a completely separate thing. Reasonable confidence is belief as man defines it. It understands with the mind. God defines belief as heart knowledge which produces living reality. This explains why so many people claim to be Christians. Their minds have comprehended God, but their hearts have not. They confess Jesus is Lord and are reasonably confident with their heart. They have God's hope and that is important; but to stop there is deadly. Matthew 7:14 states, "For the gate is narrow and the road is hard that leads to life, and there are few who find it." If we want to enter Heaven's narrow gate, we need more than a complete understanding of who Jesus is. We need to have certainty within our heart, which understands and believes beyond the recorded facts.

PRESERVING HOPE

How does one keep reasonable confidence in the things they hope? First, understand that reasonable confidence is simply the feeling that the things hoped for can be obtained. The best way to have such a feeling is to have a plan. Without a plan faith is blind. The blind are not always confident where they step. A blind man may need a guide or he is likely to stumble or fall. Likewise, having a plan is having a guide. In the Christian life, this plan should be based on God's word and promises. After we have a plan, we need to be able to trust God with that plan. Colossians 1:23 reads, "Continue securely established and steadfast in the faith, without shifting from the **hope** promised by the gospel." By having a plan and trusting God with it, no matter what the cost, hope will become certain.

THE GREATEST HOPE

The greatest expectation of hope is that of Christ's second coming. Oh, what a wonderful and glorious day that will be. It is true, that when Jesus appears the second time the world will be divided. The results of this division will be final, and for the world, it means ruin. It is equally true that there is a joyous hope in Jesus Christ for those who overcome the world. In Revelation 21:7 it reads, "Those who conquer will inherit." In the Old Testament this day is labeled as great and terrible. This day truly is great and terrible for the unbelieving, ungodly, and wicked people of this world. To those people it is a day of fearful judgment, the end of everything and everyone unholy.

For the believer this day is titled "the blessed hope" in Titus 2:13. It is a day of redemption and vindication. On this day, all those who continually believed will be assembled together to unite. In coming together they will be dressed for war and sent to battle alongside the Lord. Paul writes in 1 Thessalonians 4:16, 17 about the coming together, and Revelation 19:11-21 tells about the war. Now, when the victory is complete, and the victory is certain, then vindication will come for those who gave their lives to hold the testimony of Jesus Christ.

The resolution is the glorious completion of this "blessed hope." This is called a hope because for now it is only a dream and a vision for the believer, a glorious expectation. Believers have full assurance of this hope through the Word. It is faith that will turn this hope into living reality. Lastly, this faith can only operate by the love of God.

CHAPTER 3:

THE FAITH FACTOR

"Stand firm in your faith."
(1 Corinthians 16:13)

Become plugged into the source of eternal hope and discover eternal power. Learn where it comes from, how it works, and how to trigger it.

FAITH'S NECESSITY

Now verse 6 in Hebrews 11 reads, "Without faith it is impossible to please God." The book of James calls such a person double-minded and says that they must not expect to receive anything from the Lord (James 1:5-7). A double-minded person is a doubter. That is a very strong statement and fully worthy of examination. If a believer must possess faith to please God, then the believer should want to do all they can to attain.

MORE HOPE

The second element in faith is "conviction of things unseen." First of all, what are the things unseen? These are the same things hoped for. Romans 8:24 says, "Hope that is seen is not hope, for who hopes for what is seen?" Verse 25 adds proof by declaring, "But if we hope for what we do not see, we wait for it with patience." There it is again, a promise of patient endurance! Wait, there is more proof. Go back to verse 24. This unseen hope is the "hope we were saved in." People are not saved through hope, but through faith. Therefore, it stands to reason that the unseen things that make faith are the same things hoped for in assurance. The hope has become faith.

So faith requires a lot of sure, positive, unshaken hope. What causes this hope to become faith is a conviction of this hope. Whatever does that mean? A conviction surpasses reasonable confidence and becomes what song writer Fanny Crosby called "blessed assurance." When a person is saved, it is no longer just reasonable confidence that Jesus is Lord; it is now "blessed assurance that Jesus is mine." Having faith means that what is hoped for has just become a personal living fact and reality through a deep inner conviction. This is the belief that God requires, which involves the transformation of reasonable confidence into certainty of heart.

THE TRAVELER

Where does someone get such a conviction? If the faith is in natural things, the conviction is also natural. For example, a Eskimo is hiking on a snow covered mountain in Alaska. Along the journey he arrives at a lake. There is ice on the lake, but it only appears to be frozen on top. It would be a half-mile hike across the lake. There are tracks in the snow on top of the lake, but he is unsure of what they are. Because of the tracks he has reasonable confidence that he can walk across the ice, but he does not have faith to step on the ice. So, he takes a ten-mile hike around the lake. When he gets to the other side, he sees a light. A traveler is camped out and has a fire going. The Eskimo said to the traveler, "I was afraid to walk across the ice for fear it might break. Are those your tracks on the ice?" The traveler said, "Yes, my father gave me these special shoes and his assistant convinced me I could use them. "

If the faith is supernatural, the conviction is supernatural. Here is a supernatural explanation for this story. The Eskimo is someone who is lost without Christ. The Eskimo is unable to cross the lake because he has no conviction of what he hopes for. He only has a reasonable confidence, even though he is a native of Alaska. Now, the traveler is symbolic of the believer "who is in the world, but not of the world. Who is a light which shines in darkness" (read John 17:15 and Matthew 5:14). The reason why the traveler had faith is because his father, representing the Heavenly Father, gave him shoes which represent the gospel. Ephesians 6:15 says, "As shoes for your feet, put on whatever will make you ready to proclaim the gospel of peace." The traveler was convinced. Convincing is a mind reality. Conviction is a heart reality. Lastly, the assistant of the father is as the Bible declares, "He will give you another helper," the Holy Spirit (John 14:16). The Holy Spirit is the one who turns reasonable confidence into "blessed assurance," mind reality into heart reality.

THE SPIRIT AND THE WORD

Take a look at the Scriptures and be convinced. Hebrews 11:1b reads, "the conviction of things unseen." It has already been established that the things unseen are the same things hoped for. Also, that reasonable confidence is now "blessed assurance" because the assurance now has supernatural conviction, it is blessed. Here is the proof. To have a conviction concerning things hoped for, which are unseen, the one hoping must be convicted supernaturally. Otherwise all that one has is reasonable confidence. John 16:8 declares, "And when He comes, He will prove/convict the world wrong about sin, and righteousness, and judgment." This verse of Scripture is talking about the Holy Spirit. Therefore, it is the Holy Spirit who does the supernatural conviction of unseen things.

Is any more proof needed? Yes? Ok! Remember what happened when Abraham received conviction of unseen things concerning the number of his descendants. Genesis 15:6, "He believed the Lord." What he believed was the word the Lord revealed to him. The word of God is the vessel that conviction travels and the Spirit is the agent who convicts. Now finish Genesis 15:6, "and the Lord reckoned it to him as" what? Back to John 16:8, "And when he comes, he will prove/convict the world of" what? Both answers are "Righteousness"! The

Spirits supernatural conviction for faith is of sin, righteousness, and judgment. Abraham believed God, being fully convicted of what he hoped for. This conviction was by the Holy Spirit and was of righteousness. Although, what he hoped was believed for according to the word of God.

What he hoped was believed for according to the word of God? Remember the traveler? What he hoped was believed for according to the word of his father. His father gave him shoes. The Heavenly Father has given His children shoes, too! Their shoes are the gospel of Jesus Christ! When the shoes are on, receiving faith becomes a real possibility because then the conviction has a vessel to travel through. All the evidence is in Romans 10:17: "So faith comes from what is heard, and what is heard comes through the word of Christ."

2 Timothy 3:16 says, "All scripture is inspired by God, and is useful for teaching, for reproof, for correction, and for training in righteousness." There are two things that need to be extracted from this verse in the context of faith. One is the word reproof. The Greek word used here is *elegkron*. It is from the same Greek word used in Hebrews 11:1 translated conviction, *elegkros*. Re- is a prefix in the English language meaning again. Reproof means there is again proof or proof again. One could say that faith

is reasonable confidence of what is hoped for and proof again of that assured hope.

Secondly, notice again the presence of the Holy Spirit. "All scripture is inspired by God or God breathed." Why? To be used for "teaching, reproof, corrections, and training in righteousness." This surely sounds like a useful vessel for someone who has the assignment to "convict the world of sin, righteousness, and judgment." Does it make sense now? Conviction, reproof, "blessed assurance," whatever one names it, is all produced by God's Spirit. It's God-pleasing faith.

BY GRACE

This faith which is described in Hebrews 11 is a gift from God. Not all faith is from God, but the faith in the Bible is. That means it is purely by grace that we receive faith. Notice that faith is received. It is not taken or mustered up as some might suppose. There is nothing a person can do to achieve faith. Nothing needs to be done. Faith is a gift from the Father, paid for by the Son, with proof again through the Holy Spirit. Faith is a supernatural deposit from the Holy Spirit in the believer, the proof again of assured hope. The reason biblical faith cannot be taken or mustered is that without the gift of conviction from the Holy Spirit, we are not trusting God, we are simply hoping in God. It is true that hope is mustered up, but the conviction needed to make hope faith is only received by the Holy Spirit.

That is how salvation works. That is how faith works, even the faith for a miracle. For some reason, the hope for a miracle is much harder to believe. When belief is missing, hope becomes unsure. If a person is unsure, they begin to doubt. That is why the Holy Spirit gives us proof again. Remember what James wrote about the doubter--he should expect nothing from God. Never doubt God to stay in His graces.

Think as if the things in faith were being seen with natural eyes for a natural understanding. For example, think of God showing Abraham the stars which could not be numbered and promising him that his descendants would be as many (Genesis 15.5). This is a picture of reasonable confidence of things hoped. Faith requires conviction, a reproof. The stars were seen with his natural eyes, but the promise of descendants was made evident through the Holy Spirit. Abraham had reasonable confidence that what he desired God would perform, so he believed God without doubting. Suddenly the Holy Spirit convicts him as proof again! Now, the faith was there, but the things hoped for came in God's time. There is one thing to be certain of. Things hoped for in faith are received by grace. Remember grace is defined as "Gods undeserved favor."

Look at some of these great figures of the faith, figures like Isaac, Jacob, Moses, Rahab, Samson, and David. Isaac told the men of Gerar that his wife was his sister because he selfishly feared for his life and he favored Esau for selfish reasons. Jacob was selfish too. He swindled people left and right. He wrestled with God spiritually and physically. Moses was self absorbed, disobedient, and a murderer. Rahab was sexually loose and so were Samson and David. All six of them were given a gift in faith by a completely undeserved favor. In the case of Noah, it is spelled out in Genesis 6:8: "Noah found favor in the sight of the Lord." By grace Noah built the ark in faith and was spared from the judgment waters God flooded the Earth with. He did not take the ark or claim it in the name of Yahweh. It was purely a gift of undeserved favor.

TRY THIS!

Now that all the elements of faith have been presented, maybe it would help to paint a picture. Imagine a lamp with a long cord that is plugged in the wall. The lamp is turned on and off by a switch on the wall. Now imagine the lamp is a believer and the cord is the word of God. The believer is a light and the word is a vessel for conviction to travel. Imagine what happens if the cord is cut. The socket is the Holy

Spirit for the Spirit is the agent of conviction. Only when the switch is turned on can the power flow to a lamp. Now, imagine God is working the switch. Only when God turns the switch on can conviction flow to the believer. There is nothing the believer can do to make God turn the switch. It is purely by God's grace.

SAVING FAITH

Even though the conviction needed to make faith supernatural is purely by God's grace, Christians still have a responsibility. We are responsible to believe. Believe with the mind. James 2:19 reads, "You believe that God is one; you do well. Even the demons believe and shudder." Who were the demons? They were once angels who lived with God. They were servants of God before they fell from grace. They fell from GRACE. This happened because they chose to believe Lucifer was Who God Is. Believing God Is Who He Is, is how to receive grace If we believe that God is a Savior, He will save us. If a Healer, He will heal. If All Powerful, anything is possible.

What is the difference between demons' belief and mankind's'? The demons believe with their minds. They saw Him and knew Him as He fully is. So they are able to say with assurance through firsthand knowledge that there is one God. Mankind can only see and know Him in part. Still, if they can hope with reasonable confidence that there is one God, it is the start of faith. The next step involves believing with the mind by hearing the word of God. After the mind believes, the Holy Spirit convicts the heart and it believes. The reason the demons cannot be convicted is because they fell from grace; God cut the cord, leaving them without light.

GREATER FAITH

Just believing with the mind takes a little work when things are unseen. The work involved is not physical labor, but physical death. It is death to things seen and total dependency on God. The more persistently we offer our lives, the more God will freely turn on the switch of grace. Take a look at Luke 17:5, 6: "The apostles said to the Lord, 'Increase our faith!' The Lord replied, 'If you had faith the size of a mustard seed, you could say to this mulberry tree 'Be uprooted and planted in the sea' and it would obey you." The disciples asked Jesus for greater faith. Jesus tells them how little faith they need to see big results.

Now, read verses 7, 8, 9, and 10: "Who among you would say to your slave who has just come in from plowing or tending sheep in the field, 'come here and take your place at the table'? Would you not rather say to him, 'Prepare supper for me, put on your apron and serve me while I eat and drink; later you may eat and drink'? Do you thank the slave for doing what was commanded? So you also when you have done all that you were ordered to do, say, "We are worthless slaves; We have done only what we ought to have done!'" (NRSV)

What Jesus is saying is that although one needs little faith, they need great grace. They need a supernatural amount of "God's undeserved favor." Christians are commanded to live for Christ. If all Christians do is live for Christ, they do as they ought. They believe as they need; thus God gives to them all their needs. He turns the switch on when needed. If Christians want to see the power of God, like they read about in the Bible, they need to die for Christ that grace may increase. That requires a daily death to self. Paul talks about this in Galatians 2:20: "I have been crucified with Christ: It is no longer I who live, but Christ lives in me, and the life which I now live in the flesh I live by faith in the Son of God." The Apostle Paul decided rather to glory in his weakness with increased grace, than to pursue personal healing and glory in his flesh (see 2 Corinthians 12).

Maybe this would be an easier way to look at it. Believers are made children of God in living life more abundantly through faith in Christ Jesus. This is their duty. They are now sons and daughters. Although Jesus is the Son of God, He obediently became a servant unto death because "God so loved the world" (John 3:16). Now, this is not a commandment but it is a law. Very few sons or daughters have given up being children and put themselves last, becoming worthless slaves. The law is not to become worthless slaves. The law is that "'the last will be first and the first last." "For many are called, but few chosen. Whoever wishes to be first among you must be your slave—Just as the Son of Man came not to be served, but to serve, and to give his life a ransom for many'" (Matt. 20:16, 27, 28). So, it is not just faith that pleases God; it is the obedience that faith produces.

PERSISTANCE, PATIENT ENDURANCE, AND HUMILITY

This is how to receive supernatural, extraordinary amounts of grace. Become faithfully enslaved with God's will and watch God turn that switch. To become enslaved takes patient endurance and persistence which come from a confident hope in God. Take a look at the people Jesus healed because of their faith. Healing is a gift of grace. Many of the people who are healed today are not healed because they had great faith. Most often it is because of another's faith. God heals who He chooses and the numbers are small. If we want our faith to heal us, we need to be persistent and need to become unworthy of a miracle.

How about a few examples? First, go to Matthew Chapter 8. Read about a centurion who pleaded with Jesus for his sick servant. Jesus offered to come to his house and heal the servant. The centurion said he was unworthy, but Jesus was so impressed with his faith that He healed the servant without even seeing him.

Then in Luke Chapter 8 read about a woman with a problem with bleeding. She did not even find herself worthy to approach Jesus. Still, she was persistent enough to sneak up behind him and touch His robe. Jesus was surprised because He felt her faith. She was instantly healed and fearfully admitted what she had done. After she revealed herself, Jesus commended her for her faith and blessed her with peace.

Another great example is in Luke 18. There was a blind man begging on a road. When Jesus happened to pass by, the blind man began to cry out relentlessly for mercy. What an example of becoming unworthy. He was so persistent that no one could calm his cries. Again, healing took place and Jesus commended the man's faith.

One more healing of great faith to consider is in Matthew 15. Who can forget the Gentile woman with a possessed daughter? She knew she was unworthy, but still she asked Jesus. Jesus basically said no and compared her to a dog. This woman still begged and swallowed the shame. Jesus healed her daughter and called her faith great.

The thing to notice about these passages is that Jesus commented about the faith in these people. Although they all felt unworthy of a miracle, they each pursued Jesus with reasonable confidence that they would attain one. This appears to be the key to the grace that triggers conviction. These people died to self for a moment and received a miracle. If we desire miracles to continue, we need to persistently pursue Jesus being sure we are unworthy and can do nothing apart from God.

COST AND REWARD

Some might say that no one can pursue God unless they are drawn by the Spirit. That is very true when the purpose of pursuit is to know Him. What if the purpose of pursuit is to know Him more? Greater grace is given to those people who already know Him. The Apostle Paul most always concluded his letters urging Christians to be growing in grace. Peter concluded his second epistle strongly urging, "grow in the grace and knowledge of our Lord and Savior Jesus Christ" (2 Peter 3:18).

Salvation is a free gift of God in which there is no door for boasting. To have faith to move a mountain leaves a big door open to boast. That is why a child of God must become truly dead to self, "a worthless servant," to see God's power beyond life's needs. The Apostle Paul claimed that his infirmity was not removed by God for this very reason (see 2 Corinthians 12). When boasting is an option, God needs willfully dead people to be certain they try not to steal His glory. James Chapter 4: 5, 6 tells it this way: "God yearns jealously for the spirit that he has made to dwell in us. God opposes the proud, but gives grace to the humble." Then James instructs what needs to be done to be humbled and declares in verse 10 that who does this God "will exalt."

It is hard to except and painful to pursue God in this manner. It is so easy to ask God for miracles, but who is going to pay the price? There are few. Remember, "Many are called, but few are chosen." Those who are chosen are exalted by God. Although it costs them everything, they will be forever blessed. Whoever knows the cost, but does not make every effort to pay it, will receive severe punishment from the Lord. Luke 12:48 reads, "From everyone to whom much has been given, much will be required; and from the one to whom much has been entrusted, even more will be demanded." Whoever understands these words take caution. Remember Jonah who spent three days in the belly of a great fish because he was disobedient to what he knew to do.

What good could possibly come from knowing this? The good received from the knowledge a life of obedience to God is required. Again, salvation is free, but to be rewarded requires good works. These works give life to faith. James 2:17 reports, "Faith by itself, if it has no works, is dead." This is why "without faith it is impossible to please God, for whoever would approach him must believe that he exists and **that he rewards those who seek him**" (Hebrews 11:6).

CHAPTER 4:

THE LOVE FACTOR

"Let all that you do be done in love."
(2 Corinthians 16:14)

L earn tips on fine tuning the gift that makes faith pleasing to God and read about the Master as He demonstrates this gift.

THE GREATEST

1 Corinthians 12:31 informs us, "And I will show you a still more excellent way." 1 Corinthians 13 tells Christians that they can have supernatural, absolutely astounding, miracle-making faith, and God is oblivious to it. If love is missing, He will not even notice hope, faith, or anything else. Love is all that reaches God. Why? "For all the law is fulfilled in one word, love" (Galatians 5:14). This does not mean that there is no law. No, this means that when a heart is totally consumed with true *agape* love, evil is purged and the law does not become broken. John Wesley taught perfect love and that even a mistake is innocent when the intentions were to love.

The kind of love in God is not like the love that's in the world. God's love is pure, holy, and spotless. His love is without fault, flawless, yes altogether perfect. Therefore, it fulfills the law and all the law requires. Whatever it fails to obey, it will place a veil over. "Love covers a multitude of sins" (1 Peter 4:8).

KNOWING LOVE

What then are the characteristics of this love? To answer such a question, take a closer look at 1 Corinthians 13, verses 4 through 8.

"Love is patient." Patience is defined in Webster's dictionary as calm endurance. The best example of patience is God's calm endurance with the sinner "not wanting that any should perish, but all to come to repentance" (2 Peter 3:9). Likewise, Christians should calmly endure all people, all things, and all circumstances.

"Love is kind." A perfect example of kindness is the way Jesus says to treat one's enemies (Luke 6:27-31). Do good to them, blessing them, and praying for them. Calmly receive their abuse physically and emotionally without defense, giving to them freely. Showing kindness to the unkind is to "heap burning coals on their heads" (Romans 12:20).

"Love is not envious or boastful or arrogant or rude." All four of these adjectives are similar in the sense that they all stem from pride. The thing to notice here is where this pride is rooted. Envy is of the will. Boastful is of the mind. Arrogance is of the heart. Rudeness is of the body. Remember to "love the Lord your God with all your heart, mind, will, and strength" (see Luke 10:27).

"Love does not insist on its own way." Hardest of all is not insisting on oneself. This means submission, understanding, and self denial. John 5:30 tells us, "I seek not to do my will but the will of Him who sent me." Jesus never insisted on His own way. Rather,

He offered Himself as the way and is patiently waiting for followers.

"Love is not irritable or resentful." This does not mean that love does not get mad or feel pain. No, love can become burning angry and the pain reaches very deep. Love can even hate. What? That's right. "God is love and there are six things He hates" (Proverbs 6:16). Be very careful on the day it does come to cool it off before the night falls. If anger is left to burn all night long, the pain of resentment becomes very bitter. Ephesians 4:26 states, "Be angry, and do not sin; do not let the sun go down on your wrath."

"Love does not rejoice in wrong-doing, but rejoices in the truth." This seems like a pretty cut and dried statement, but is it? One thing to notice is that this verse does not read love rejoices in the good. It reads "rejoices in the truth." Why, because the truth is not always good. Jesus said that He is the truth in John 14:6. Jesus also said that only God is good in Matthew 19:17. The truth can be very ugly sometimes, but there is freedom in knowing the truth. "The truth will make you free" (John 8:32).

"Love bears all things." This word comes from the Greek, *stego*, which means to cover or to conceal. Try to picture Jesus as He bears the sins of the world. Not as in exposing or revealing the sins, but as in covering or concealing the sins with His shed blood. That is true *agape* love.

"Love believes all things, hopes all things, and endures all things." There are so many truths to find in these characteristic of love. For the purposes of faith, just consider these final three verbs. According to *Webster's Dictionary*, to believe is to take as true. Hope is to feel that what is wanted will happen. To endure means to last or continues to stand. If these definitions are fitted together, then love takes as true feeling that what is wanted will happen and continues to stand. Does that sound like the assurance of things hoped for?

"Love never ends." How can anyone say that love never ends? First of all, this love that never ends is not the love of friends, family, or even husband and wife. This is the love of God, *agape* love. God is eternal, having no beginning and no end. 1 John 4:8 declares, "God is love." Thus, "love never ends." This love is available to all who believe through faith in Christ Jesus. The demons put their faith in Lucifer and so they fell from grace. They are no longer entitled to God's *agape* love.

NO GREATER GIFT

Mankind is given great grace with faith. Again, 1 John 4:8 declares, "God is love." He loves everyone as a father loves his children. This is a family type of love and it will end. *Agape* love never ends. Romans 8:38, 39 declares the power of this love. "For I am convinced that neither death, nor life, nor angels, nor rulers, nor things present, nor things to come, nor powers, nor height, nor depth, nor anything else in all creation, will be able to separate us from the **love of God** in Christ Jesus our lord. There it is, *agape* love. Love that never ends! This love is in the Lord Jesus Christ." That is the key. God loves everyone. "God is love." Unless we have the love of God in Christ Jesus, we will be separated from God for all eternity.

Back to 1 Corinthians 13; the first three verses describe great acts of service to God that are performed without love. Things like healing the sick, feeding the poor, even becoming a martyr. It remarks that all these things are non-existing to God because love is absent. Imagine the consequences. Matthew 7:23 shares the consequences. "Then I will declare to them, 'I never knew you; depart from me, you evildoers.'" Why are these judged so harshly? Did these not serve with great power and authority? Yes, they did great things, but the Father was blind to all them. It was not what they did that was evil. It was how they did it. They did it with impure motives. Motives that were lacking the greatest gift, love.

This love is not an emotion. There is no need for warm or harmonious feelings. This love is a choice and decision to live patient, kind, and all the other characteristics mentioned earlier. Before, the choice or decision is made to live this life, Jesus needs to be Lord in our hearts and not just our minds. They could call Him Lord in Matthew 7:21, but by verse 23 Jesus says He never knew them.

AN EXAMPLE OF LOVE

No one was as great of an example of this love as Lord Jesus. One of the best illustrations of Jesus choosing to live *agape* love is found in John chapter 8. Verse 1 reads, "While Jesus went to the Mount of Olives." This verse just tells where Jesus spent the night. What He did on the mount is not mentioned, but Jesus was often known to withdraw from the crowds of people for time to pray. Taking time to cover everything in prayer is a beautiful picture of love bearing all things.

Verse 2 states, "Early in the morning he came again to the temple. All the people came to him and he sat down and began to teach them." Jesus did not waste any time. He did not arrive at the temple mid- morning or late morning. Persistence and perseverance are evidence of love that endures all things. Every characteristic, patience, kindness, not envy or boast...All of them are necessary to be a effective minister of the Word.

Next, in verses 3 and 4, "The scribes and Pharisees brought a woman who had been caught in adultery; and making her stand before all of them, they said to him, 'Teacher, this woman was caught in the very act of adultery.'" It is clear that the love of God is not in the scribes and Pharisees. First, their actions here are boastful, arrogant, and rude toward Jesus' teaching. They were clearly insisting on their own way and rejoicing in the woman's wrongdoing. They now have the nerve to say in verse 5, "'In the law Moses commanded us to stone such women. Now what do you say?'" Here is where envy enters the picture. They are envying the law, for they are angry and provoked with evil resentment toward Jesus.

Verse 6 makes this perfectly clear. "They said this to test him, so that they might have some charge to bring against him." Their anger and resentment toward Jesus has devised an evil plan of entrapment. This gave them greater desire to rejoice in wrongdoing. The law as Moses commanded is also truth. What a perfect example of how the truth is not always good. Finishing verse 6, "Jesus bent down and wrote with his finger on the ground." What Jesus wrote is only speculated. Some say He was stalling for time and waiting for the Father's words. If this theory is true it shows that love is patient. Others say that He was trying to avoid the question altogether. If this is true then it shows love does not rejoice in wrong doing and again that love bears all things or always protects. Possibly, He wrote a new commandment on the ground, John 15:8, "This is my commandment that you love one another.'"

There are many other opinions as to what Jesus wrote on the ground that day. The scriptural focus here is not on what Jesus wrote. The focus is simply on the action Jesus took in response to the question. No matter how it is looked at, the action taken is one of love. This becomes more and more evident as the story continues.

The story continues in John 8:7, "When they kept on questioning him, he straightened up and said to them, "'Let anyone among you who is without sin be the first to throw a stone at her.'" First, notice the loveless action of the scribes and Pharisees. Not only did they hate the woman they had caught, but they were being continually hateful toward Jesus by nagging Him to answer. When Jesus finally answered, what incredible love is expressed. All the characteristics of *agape* are present in this response. Think about how easy it would have been for Jesus to have lost His temper at this point, but love is not irritable or resentful. Jesus had found a higher truth to rejoice in. Romans 3:23 records this truth; "All have sinned and fall short of the glory of God." Through patient endurance for this truth, Jesus has removed the question about what this woman has done and made the question about what they have done. He did this by hoping and believing in the truth.

Now, take a look at verse 8: "And once again he bent down and wrote on the ground." Notice that the focus again is not on what is written. The focus continues to be on Jesus' action. What is His action showing about love now? He has answered the question and reversed the accusation. Clearly, now is the time for a victory dance! Yes, love rejoices in the truth, but it does not rejoice in wrong doing. So, rather than boasting or insisting on His own way, Jesus kindly allows them to select judgment after sharing the truth. Another option could have been for Jesus to have condemned the scribes and Pharisees at this point. This too would have negated His purpose. John 3:17 reads, "Indeed, God did not send the Son into the world to condemn the world, but in order that the world might be saved through him."

Reading verse 9 now, "When they heard it, they went away, one by one, beginning with the elders; and Jesus was left alone with the woman standing before him." This is a perfect picture that love never ends or never fails. God's love quickly shut down their evil plan to test Jesus. All concern over this woman's immoral act was suddenly covered up. For love again bears all things. Verse 10 only reinforces this. "Jesus straightened up and said to her, 'Woman, where are they? Has no one condemned you?'" One can only imagine the compassion and tenderness with which Jesus spoke these words, for love is kind.

Beginning with her response, Verse 11 reads, "She said, 'No one, sir.'" Her answer was quite calm and respectful for someone who was just about to be stoned. One might expect her response to be more fearful. This is a testimony to the perfect love of God. 1 John 4:18 declares, "There is no fear in love, but perfect love cast out fear and whoever fears has not reached perfection in love." Now, 1 John 4:19 reads, "We love because he first loved us." Jesus won this woman with God's unconditional love, *agape*. Now, as He continues to love her, He says, "'Neither do I condemn you. Go your way, and from now on do not sin again.'" These are the greatest words of love a sinner could ever hear. In these final words of loving kindness, Jesus has covered her sin, given her hope, faith to believe, and instruction to endure.

Something must be said about the instruction to endure. This is very closely tied with the good works needed to receive increased grace for greater faith. Good works are a product of God's love which is pure. 1 John 5:3, 4 reads, "For the love of God is this, that we obey his commandments. And his commandments are not burdensome, for whatever is born of God conquers the world. And this is the victory that conquers the world, our faith." What John is saying is that someone born again has faith to move mountains. Remember a mustard seed is all one needs. It is the love of God that brings obedience which makes faith pleasing to God. If love is gone, then even faith is invisible to God. Therefore, love is a "more excellent way" (1 Corinthians 12:31).

CHAPTER 5:

TESTIMONY

"The only thing that counts is faith working through love."

(Galatians 5:6)

Read about a dream come true; a story of God turning the switch. As a teenager I prayed for a beautiful, God-fearing, Asian wife.

AND IT WAS GOOD

Here is a true story of God-pleasing faith in the present. There was a young woman who was born and raised in the Philippines. She had a comfortable living and high education in the field of accounting. She already had an accounting position with a large soda company and great potential for promotion. More than even all that, she was very beautiful to behold and many men desired her. Although she had everything going her way, she was still missing a certain peace. She was a born-again Christian and felt that God had something better for her.

She had a dream that she would meet her husband at a football game. Football is not played in the Philippines. She felt that her husband must be in another land, so she applied for a visa. When she received a visa to visit Canada she was very excited. She instantly thought that her future husband must be in Canada. Immediately, she made plans to visit her uncle who lived in Alberta, Canada. To her surprise she also was granted a visa to visit the U.S. She thought nothing of it, but still made plans to spend three days with a cousin living in San Francisco, California.

While she was in Canada, several men courted her and one even proposed, but she never had peace about any of them. Her vacation was almost over and she was ready to go home. Only one week remained when she was reading her e-mail. A pop-up screen appeared advertising a Christian matching service. It was an interesting site and it was offering a free one-week trial. So, she logged on out of curiosity. When she logged on, she had to create a profile. She answered the questions but never added her picture to the profile. Only one man replied to her profile. His profile scared her. He wrote that before Christ he was a wild man. This man would drink, party, and cause trouble. Then he got into a car accident and was disabled because of it. He also had no job and lived with his mother. Surely this man was not God's choice for her, but she answered his reply thinking that maybe he could be a friend. This man was seeking the wife God had for him. He did not want to get involved with the wrong woman. After he had the accident, he became an on-fire Christian. About a year earlier, he went through a bad relationship which had left a terrible mark on his relationship with God. During this relationship he was able, by God's grace, to graduate college with a degree in Bible/Theology. All this man wanted to do was please God, but he felt that he had made such a mess of his life. He had no idea what this girl looked like, but he had a reasonable confidence that she was God's choice for him.

He asked her if she could visit the U.S. She told him about her plans to visit her cousin for just three days. With even greater assurance, he invited her to come and see him. She said that she would pray about it, but she had no more money. In faith, he e-mailed her a musical e-card which played, "God Will Make A Way." Then he said he was going away to Canada for revival over the weekend and asked her to seek God about whether she should come or not. Los Angeles is about 2000 miles from where he lived. As he went to Canada, she flew to Los Angeles. While she was in the air, she felt the Lord speak to her and said, go to Pittsburgh. Fearing God, she e-mailed him what she believed God spoke and said she would come see him if she could find an available flight.

There it is, proof again. Convicted now, he offered to buy her a plane ticket and book the flight. He had no job and his only income was disability from the government, but he was convicted within that she was God's choice for him. She was very surprised that he did that when he had never even seen her. That was on a Monday. Tuesday, God provided an opening to board a flight leaving Wednesday from Los Angeles to Pittsburgh for less than $200 roundtrip. What a blessing!

As she was on the plane to Pittsburgh, God spoke to her through His word from the book of Ruth. This is the word she received. "For wherever you go, I will go; And wherever you lodge, I will lodge. Your people shall be my people, And your God my God" (Ruth 1:16). This word struck fear in her and she began to cry. When she finally met this man, she was frightened by his appearance. He had a beard which is very uncommon in the Philippines. When He saw her he was quite surprised to behold her beauty.

The next two days they became increasingly attracted to each other. By the third day, he had proposed to her. Then she remembered the word she got from Ruth and agreed to marry him. That night she became very scared and she began to plan to leave. First thing Saturday morning, she began praying and seeking God for clear direction. Then she got another word from the Lord, warning her not to flee like the prophet Jonah. Remembering that Jonah was swallowed by a big fish for running from God, she quickly decided to stay and kept these things to herself. He got a job bagging groceries as she began to plan their wedding. Four months later they got married. They have been married five years now, have two beautiful children, and they own their own home.

Times have not always been easy, and they have had disagreements. The disagreements have been largely due to cultural differences, but their love is based on a decision and not just feelings and emotion. Sure, they do have strong feelings for each other, but when cultures clash and feelings are hurt, their love never ends. So God continues to bless them and they continue to hope in him in "faith working through love" every day (Galatians 5:6).

CHAPTER 6:

CALL TO REACTION

> "For though by this time you ought to be teachers, you need someone to teach you again."
>
> (Hebrews 5:12)

Now is the time to mature in Christ. Times are becoming more and more evil every day. It is becoming increasingly harder for people to choose life. Many of those who have chosen life are in danger of becoming lukewarm. Jesus warns the lukewarm Christians that "I am about to spit you out of my mouth" (Revelation 3:16).

ACT NOW

There are four ways a reader can react to this book. First, they can choose to close the book and ignore the truth. The truth is that judgment is coming and the world is being divided. How comfortable a life entangled in the ignorance and pleasures of sin can be. Sorry to ring the bell, but the end is ruin. The scriptures say that there is pleasure in sin for a season. As winter turns to spring, spring turns to summer and so on; so this pleasure will turn to sorrow.

How many times must the cycle continue? How many nights must one enjoy the pleasure of sin just to wake up time and time again saying, "Life is a joke" or "Somebody shoot me"? There are so many negative catch phrases for a miserable overworked life. When are people going to believe Jesus' words in Mathew 11:28, "Come to me, all you who are weary and are heavy burdens, and I will give you rest."

A second option is to continue being content with the reasonable confidence that comes from merely the head knowledge of Christ. This is probably the most common response to any message of God by today's so-called Christians. These people understand that sin will destroy. They have been fully convinced, largely because they have suffered or know someone else who has suffered the effects of sin. They have knowledge but lack understanding.

As a result, they cease to sin when it is obvious. Still they hold on to sins that they are comfortable with or there is minimal direct consequence as a result. Sure some people are waiting on deliverance and for them there is grace. A greater number of these people know the truth and the truth has set them free, but they will not step out of their prison. The Lord has broken the shackles from their ankles, but they will not shake them off. 1 Peter 2:9 says that God "called you out of darkness into his marvelous light."

This is a dangerous way to live the Christian life. Hebrews 10:26 reads, "For if we willfully persist in sin after having received the knowledge of the truth, there no longer remains a sacrifice for sins." This is referring to the blood of Jesus. This is not referring to sins of ignorance or error, but this is direct disobedience of a person who is fully aware. Ignorance or error will not erase the guilt of sins committed toward God, but it does permit grace to abound. It is this place of grace that His mercy flows through the blood of Jesus. After one has been fully enlightened, grace no longer remains. Willful sin should no longer exist in a believer. A true Christian is expected to remain in Christ as the result of the new birth. 1 John 3:9 reads, "Those who have been born of God do not sin, they cannot sin." This verse does not mean that sin is no longer possible. No, this means that the desire to sin is gone and the power of sin has been destroyed. There is freedom in Christ

Jesus, freedom to no longer sin. 1 Peter 2:16 instructs us, "live as free people, yet do not use your freedom as a pretext for evil."

Now that you have been enlightened, cry out to the Holy Spirit in the name of Jesus for the conviction that "cuts to the heart" (Acts 2:37). This is a third and better option. Admit to God that His grace has been trampled on by willful sin. Tell Him that He deserves better. Then as Jesus told the woman who was caught in adultery, after He saved her, "Go your way, and from now on do not sin again" (John 8:11).

Finally, maybe the cord is plugged in the socket, but the lamp is only giving off 15, 25, or even 60 watts of light. Increase the wattage by seeking God's undeserved favor. In other words seek to become fully enlightened. This choice is not for everyone. James 3:1 reads, "Not many of you should become teachers, my brothers and sisters, for you know that we who teach will be judged with greater strictness." Let each person be convicted as to how far they are to go in spiritual things.

Although all should not desire to be fully enlightened, all are instructed to "go on toward perfection, leaving behind the basic teaching, if God permits" (Hebrews 6:1, 4). No believer should become a spiritual sloth or become stagnant. It is when Christians do this that God's grace begins to abound and the miraculous increases in their daily lives. God is not thrift in giving. Do not seek His graces cheaply or casually.

One final warning--stay alert of those whose lamps appear to give off 100 watts, but actually only 15 watts are truly in use. Matthew 10:15 warns us, "Beware of false prophets." Take this warning seriously, for the days are evil. Whatever it costs, now is the time to become mature in Christ. 1 Peter 5:10 promises, "And after you have suffered for a little while, the God of all grace, who has called you to his eternal glory in Christ, will himself restore, support, strengthen, and establish you." Therefore, do not be deceived by those who teach you of an easier or more comfortable way. Philippians 2:12 directs us, "Work out your own salvation with fear and trembling."

Printed in the United States
209638BV00001B/1-393/P